"Go and make disciples of all nations, baptizing them in the name of the Father and of the Son and of the Holy Spirit, and teaching them to obey all that I have commanded you" (Matt. 28:19–20).

The Great Commission encompasses the whole task of the church. And here is help for fulfilling that task—the DISCIPLING RESOURCES series. Designed for small-group use, whether Bible study, Sunday school, or fellowship groups, this effective approach is firmly based on biblical principles of disciple building.

Each group member receives his or her own copy of the book, which guides the group through thirteen weekly meetings. Every step of the group- and personal-study process is included, plus biblical material and commentary. Leaders need only facilitate participation. This series is designed to increase knowledge of God's Word, cultivate supportive personal relationships, and stimulate spiritual growth—an adventure in being His disciples.

Titles in this exciting new series:

Available now	Projected
Basic Christian Values	*Being Christ's Church (Ephesians)*
First Steps for New and Used Christians	*Discipling Your Emotions*
	Developing Personal Responsibility
Fruit of the Spirit	*A Life of Fellowship (1 John)*
The Good Life (Rom. 12–16)	

BASIC CHRISTIAN VALUES

LARRY RICHARDS
NORM WAKEFIELD

ZONDERVAN PUBLISHING HOUSE

OF THE ZONDERVAN CORPORATION
GRAND RAPIDS, MICHIGAN 49506

BASIC CHRISTIAN VALUES
© 1981 by The Zondervan Corporation

Library of Congress Cataloging in Publication Data

Richards, Lawrence O
    Basic Christian values.

    (Discipling resources)
    1. Christian ethics—Study and teaching. 2. Values—Study
and teaching. I. Wakefield, Norm, joint author. II. Title. III. Series.

BJ1251.R47   241   80-27853
ISBN 0-310-43421-1

Scripture passages are from the Holy Bible: New International
Version. Copyright © 1978 by the New York International Bible
Society. Used by permission.

Edited by Mary Bombara

Printed in the United States of America

CONTENTS

WHAT'S IMPORTANT TO ME 1

The simplest definition of a "value" is "something that is *important to me."* When a person says, "Time to read is important to me" or, "It's important to me that you get good grades in school," he or she is making a statement about values.

In the first three meetings together you and the rest of your discipling group will explore the nature and the function of values. On that base you'll move on to examine several basic Christian values.

We can think about Christian value as something that is important to *God.* As Christians we want our feelings and ideas about what is important in life to match His.

Usually, though, for all of us, the first values we adopt are our parents' values. Mom and dad are the first transmitters of values . . . we gain our first impression of what's important from them.

So, think back together, and compare. What were some of the values you learned from *your* parents?

LIST

What was
really important
to my father?

_____

_____

_____

_____

_____

_____

_____

_____

_____

_____

_____

_____
_____
_____
_____
_____
_____
_____
_____
_____
_____
_____

LIST

What was
really important
to my mother?

SHARE
with each other
in groups
of six.

What three values were *most important* to my father?

What three values were *most important* to my mother?

SELECT

one word that describes the relationship between your mother's and father's values. In your group of six tell each other the word and describe the impact of this situation on you, if any.

"Comparing mom's and dad's values, I believe they were . . .

___UNIFORM   ___HARMONIOUS

___DIFFERENT   ___CONFLICTING

LIST

here at least
ten values
you presently hold.
(That is,
things that are
important to
you now.)

_____ _____

_____ _____

_____ _____

_____ _____

_____ _____

_____ _____

_____ _____

_____ _____

_____ _____

_____ _____

ANALYZE

Look at the list
and place by each item . . .

X   if the value is similar to one of your parents' values.

O   if the value is distinctly yours and was not held by your parents.

↔   if the value is in *conflict* with values held by your parents.

PREDICT

Now divide each group of six into groups of three . . .

Have one group member share one personal value from the list on p. 12. The other group members must then predict whether this value is similar to, different from, or in conflict with the person's parents' values.

Repeat this process until each group member has shared three of his or her personal values. (If possible choose one of each type:**x**, **o** or **↔** .)

Then close this session in prayer.

INSIGHT

Each week *after* the group session you'll be given the opportunity to think back and gain insight into yourself, your values, and the patterns of your own life. Do take time to work through the areas suggested for INSIGHT exploration. Reflecting on what you have done and studied is one key to effective learning.

1 What did you learn about your parents? _____

_____

_____

_____

_____

_____

2 What have you learned about your parents' impact on your life?

_____

_____

_____

_____

_____

3 What have you learned about your own values? _____

_____

_____

_____

_____

_____

4 What insights do you have into the setting in which values are

communicated? _____

_____

_____

_____

_____

_____

EXPLORING PERSONAL VALUES 2

Values can be known or hidden; consciously held, or expressed in behavior without our even being aware of their existence!

Research has shown that many people live without ever understanding the values that are reflected in their daily choices. While this is not necessarily "bad" or "wrong," it is helpful for us all to have insight into ourselves and our values. The more we understand ourselves and the things we hold important, the better able we are to open our lives to the work of God's Spirit in transforming our values.

Values are not fixed and unchangeable. Some values that we uncover *we* may want to change, as a key to our personal growth.

Quiz

Fill out the following questionnaire.

On the left, mark each item: SA (strongly agree), A (agree), ? (uncertain), D (disagree), SD (strongly disagree).

___ 1. An immature believer will need to receive, while a mature believer will be able to give. ___

___ 2. One ought to measure "success" by growth in self and others. ___

___ 3. We ought to protect others from making mistakes. ___

___ 4. Playing with children is a family priority. ___

___ 5. Our use of money shows what is important to us. ___

___ 6. It is demeaning to accept charity. ___

___ 7. It is wrong to want to be a success on earth. ___

___ 8. A healthy individual should desire freedom. ___

___ 9. If a person is not growing he is falling short of God's intention for him. ___

___ 10. Everyone should put away 15% of his income for future emergencies. ___

___ 11. Work should have greater significance in life than leisure. ___

___ 12. It is more important for parents to build a loving relationship with children than to require obedience. ___

___ 13. There are some opportunities that are too great to miss out on, no matter how old a person is. ___

___ 14. One should take care of himself first, so he has energy to serve others. ___

___ 15. We have a right to be generous with others instead of being ___ merely fair.

___ 16. When a person begins to fail, others should step in and take ___ over.

___ 17. The accomplishments that give us the greatest pleasure ___ indicate our view of success.

___ 18. In our society, wealth is a valid way to measure importance. ___

___ 19. It is more spiritual to give than to receive. ___

___ 20. We ought to treat all others equally and fairly. ___

___ 21. We should always live for eternity and not be concerned ___ with the present.

___ 22. A person needs a college education to be a success in life. ___

___ 23. Parents should make sure their children make right ___ choices.

___ 24. We should teach our children to pull their own weight. ___

___ 25. Having hobbies is nice but unimportant. ___

___ 26. A Christian should live in the present and never be con- ___ cerned for the future.

___ 27. Normally God will give faithful believers material blessings. ___

___ 28. God wants His children to prosper financially. ___

___ 29. A person should be willing to take risks. ___

___ 30. A Christian ought always to serve others and not consider ___ his own needs.

___ 31. People who learn to live within their limitations are admi- ___ rable.

___ 32. A Christian should give more than he receives. ___

QUIZ
continued

___ 33. One should work hard to provide his or her family with ___
   extras.

___ 34. A Christian must always give priority to the financial security ___
   of his family.

___ 35. A person who makes wise decisions will always consider the ___
   future outcome.

___ 36. It's only right to work for what we get in life. ___

___ 37. A successful person grasps every opportunity without ___
   hesitating.

___ 38. It is better to be wealthy than poor. ___

___ 39. People who relax easily are probably lazy. ___

___ 40. One ought not to tackle more than he is sure he can handle. ___

GO BACK OVER THE QUIZ, AND

on the right, mark each item: C (characterizes the kind of person I am), B (describes the kind of person I am becoming), D (does not describe me).

Note: There is no "answer key" of "right" or "wrong" answers to this questionnaire. Instead the questions and your responses will help you explore a variety of values in the weeks ahead.

CHECK

The questions just completed are designed to explore values in eight areas. Check the area which is most important to you right now.

_____ Success vs. "Success"

_____ Fairness vs. Grace

_____ Work vs. Leisure

_____ Serving vs. Being Served

_____ Present vs. Future

_____ Growth vs. Conformity

_____ Freedom vs. Control

_____ People vs. Possessions

SHARE

in groups of six
the answers you gave
to the quiz questions
pertaining to in the area
you checked (p. 21).

Fairness vs. Grace

Questions 6, 15, 20, 24, and 36 deal with the value area of fairness vs. grace. If this is the area you checked share your answers to these questions.

Work vs. Leisure

Questions 4, 11, 25, 33, and 39 deal with the value area of work vs. leisure. If this is the area you checked share your answers to these questions.

Serving vs. Being Served

Questions 1, 14, 19, 30, and 32 deal with the value area of serving vs. being served. If this is the area you checked share your answers to these questions.

Success vs. "Success"

Questions 2, 7, 17, 22, and 27 deal with the value area of success vs. "success." If this is the area you checked share your answers to these questions.

Growth vs. Conformity

Questions 9, 13, 29, 31, and 40 deal with the value area of growth vs. conformity. If this is the area you checked share your answers to these questions.

Freedom vs. Control

Questions 3, 8, 12, 16, and 23 deal with the value area of freedom vs. control. If this is the area you checked share your answers to these questions.

Present vs. Future

Questions 10, 21, 26, 35, and 37 deal with the value area of present vs. future. If this is the area you checked share your answers to these questions.

People vs. Possessions

Questions 5, 18, 28, 34, and 38 deal with the value area of people vs. possessions. If this is the area you checked share your answers to these questions.

Share also the answers
to these questions:

1 Were the items easy or difficult to answer?
2 What else about this value/area concerns you now?
3 In what ways does this issue affect your life now?

DISCUSS
in your group of six

Is there any kind of conflict between your values and the values of your parents in the area you just selected and talked about?

FINALLY

Pray with and for each other as you conclude.

INSIGHT

1 Write down by the values areas on pages 22 and 23 the name of individuals in your group of six who chose it. Pray during the week for each, focusing your prayers on each one's area.

2 Summarize the most significant personal insight gained in this time together.

_____

_____

_____

_____

3 How many "strongly agree" responses did you make on the forty questions? _____

How many "characterizes me" responses did you make on the forty questions? _____

What conclusions might you draw from this comparison?

_____

_____

_____

_____

CHOOSING VALUES

Earlier we said that a value is something that is "important to me." Now we want to expand that understanding. A *significant* value is something which is *important enough to find consistent expression in the choices I make.* The true test of values is not in our words of agreement, but in our lifestyle and actions.

We saw earlier that values can be shaped through the influences of others who are significant to us. Values, it is often said, are "caught" rather than taught. But values are not static, changeless things. Values grow and change as we grow and change. Also, values are not *determined* . . . what our parents have done will not shape us unchangeably, for good or for evil.

Yes, we do have freedom to *choose* our own values. We can evaluate what is important, make our own determinations, and then go on to live by principles we have chosen to be our own.

We can choose to live by God's values.

ROLE PLAY

Take the parts of persons in this
Sunday school class and read the script
with feeling.

JACK: Today, class, we're going to focus on how important it is that we defend the truth that the Bible is the inerrant, inspired, completely trustworthy Word of God. But before we begin . . . yes, Carl?

CARL: Jack, we all know the Bible's trustworthy. And we spent last Sunday on that subject, too.

JACK: But today, Carl, the Bible is under attack. We must know how to defend it when godless or deceived individuals . . .

CAROL: Jack, I really respect your commitment to the Bible. But I wonder if you heard what Carl was saying. I have the feeling he has some other concern—maybe something personal—that he wishes we'd explore together.

JACK: Of course, I don't want to ignore Carl's feelings, Carol. It's just that our view of the Bible is one of the most important issues in a Christian's life.

CAROL: But it's not the only issue.

JACK: No. But . . .

CAROL: What do some of the rest of you think? What are some of the important issues we ought to study in our class?

CARL: I think the Bible is an important issue. It's just that Jack, you've had us working on that study for six months. Now, I'd like to have some studies of, oh, say how a Christian should use his money.

ANN: And how about time? I heard somewhere that each of us has just 24 hours a day, and we need to use it wisely. What about you, Carol?

CAROL: Oh, I guess one thing I think is important is people.

ANN: People? How do you mean?

CAROL: Well, like just now I felt that Jack—I know you didn't mean it this way, Jack—was sort of ignoring Carl's concerns. I think that respecting other people, seeing their needs first, sort of, is very important. And God talks a lot about that in the Bible.

ANN: Yes, that's important, all right. But so is our use of time. I wish my husband wouldn't spend so much time at work. He never agrees when I want to go out for dinner or to have friends over. Why, he's even working this morning.

CARL: Ann, maybe that's because of Ed's commitment to stewardship. After all, he has a lot of people working for him. And I know he gives a lot of money to missions.

ANN: Well, maybe. Actually I think he works just because he likes to. He's a workaholic, if you know what I mean.

JACK: Well, I'll tell you. What bothers me is that every one of the problems you want to talk about has answers in the Bible. But if no one trusts their Bible, who'll ever find the answer? I think we've got to be *sure* we know what we believe about the inerrancy of the Bible.

CARL: OK, Jack. But you've convinced us already. That's why we want to go on to something new.

ANN: I sure wish my husband could come to a study on putting the right priorities on his time.

CARL: Personally, I'd like to explore what the Bible says about money. You know, if I do sell that patent, I might have several hundred thousand dollars a year income soon. I'd like to have some plan laid out on how to invest it and spend it and how much to give, and things like that.

CAROL: Carl, I think it's wonderful that you have all that inventive talent. I sure hope you do sell the patent.

CARL: Thanks, Carol. And I sure wish you'd all help me work through how to use all that money in a godly way, if it comes.

CAROL: Well, Carl, I hope you'll use it to meet real human needs, and not just to put up a building or something. Every human being has so much potential, and I believe the Lord wants to see every bit realized.

ANN: And I believe husbands ought to plan their time to be sure wives and children feel loved.

JACK: And I believe the time is up. And say, gang. Let's get back to the inerrancy of Scripture next week. We really wasted a lot of time just talking today.

ANALYSIS

Together in groups of six
agree on how to complete
the column.

PERSON	WHAT VALUE OR VALUES ARE EXPRESSED?
JACK "We must know how to defend the Bible." "The answers to your problems are in the Bible. If no one trusts the Bible, how will they ever find the answers?"	
CAROL "One thing I think is important is people." "Use money to meet real human needs." "Every human being has so much potential."	
CARL "I'd like to study how a Christian should use his money." "I might have hundreds of thousands next year . . . how should I invest or spend it?" "How can I use money in a godly way?"	
ANN "We need to use our time wisely." "I wish my husband wouldn't spend so much time at work." "I wish he could come to a study on putting the right priorities on time."	

LIST

together as many ways you can think
of that each person's *expressed value*
might show up in his or her behavior.

LIKELY BEHAVIORS

ANALYSIS

Expressed values (the things we *say* are important to us) may or may not show up as a *way of life.*

Look *behind the scenes* at each character in the play. Decide together if the value *expressed in words* is *truly* important to each individual. Circle your answer.

JACK

Jack studies many books about the Bible these days. He underlines, makes notes, and becomes very angry when an author disagrees with his point of view.

Jack himself does little devotional reading of the Bible. He sees his all-consuming passion to gather evidence to defend Scripture as his calling from God, and seems to feel no need for other kinds of study or exploration of Scripture.

Jack's lifestyle described above *is/is not* in harmony with the value he says he holds concerning Scripture. (Circle one.)

We might conclude that Jack's values related to Scripture are (a) expressed values only . . . verbal but not acted on, (b) lived values as well as expressed, or (c) values held inconsistently, having an impact on his life in some areas but not applied appropriately in others. (Circle one.)

CAROL

Carol often speaks up to check on how others are thinking or feeling. She gives generously of her time for many projects, and also leads a troop of Girl Scouts at a school for retarded children. Carol is very sensitive to her children and finds time daily to talk with each individually about school and other activities.

Carol's lifestyle *is/is not* in harmony with her expressed values.

Carol's values related to persons are (a) expressed only, (b) lived as well as expressed, or (c) held inconsistently, applied to some areas but not others.

ANN

Ann is a night person who enjoys staying up and reading in her quiet, dark home till 3 or 4 A.M. She gets up at noon, because her husband takes care of breakfast for the kids before he goes to work. She resents planning ahead, feeling that only spontaneous action is meaningful.

Ann's lifestyle *is/is not* in harmony with her expressed values.

Ann's values related to time are (a) expressed only, (b) lived as well as expressed, or (c) held inconsistently, applied to some areas but not others.

CARL

Carl lives comfortably with his wife, who works as a nurse. They have three cars, two boats, and a travel trailer, along with a house full of modern labor-saving and other appliances. Carl has two savings accounts—one for money for his inventions, and one for "emergencies." He enjoys talking about how he will use his money for the Lord when he gets rich.

Carl's lifestyle *is/is not* in harmony with his expressed values.

Carl's values related to money are (a) expressed only, (b) lived as well as expressed, or (c) held inconsistently, applied to some areas but not to others.

A Word from Norm

It's a popular error to confuse *beliefs* with *values*. A person may very well say, "I believe we should love our neighbor," and we are likely to take this as an expression of his values. But the belief may not express a value at all.

How can we tell? We'll know if we watch him for a while. He drives off to work while his neighbor struggles with a flat tire. He allows his dogs to bark constantly, keeping the neighbors awake at night. He neglects the care of his yard, making the neighborhood less desirable. Actions like these suggest that while he may profess belief in loving our neighbors, loving them is not truly important to him.

A *value* is something that is actually *important enough to be expressed in my daily choices.*

This helps us in thinking about the nature and the role of values in our own lives. There are certain things that we recognize, or believe, *are* important (loving our neighbor, using time wisely, whatever). But then daily life brings us to points at which *choices* must be made. We choose either to do, or not to do, as our belief suggests. When I keep on making choices that express what I have said I believe is important so it becomes part of the habit of life I am building, then it is a significant value.

How good it is to recognize, and put into practice, this simple process of growth toward godliness.

I discover or state what I believe to be important.

As opportunities come I choose daily to act on what I believe is important.

As I consistently make such choices, the belief becomes part of my character and lifestyle.

And *then* it is truly a value to me . . . important enough to me to be consistently expressed in daily choices.

VALUES CHOICE ANALYSIS

In your group of six,
analyze these two typical
experiences of Daniel.

But Daniel resolved not to defile himself with the royal food and wine, and he asked the chief official for permission not to defile himself this way. Now God had caused the official to show favor and sympathy to Daniel, but the official told Daniel, "I am afraid of my lord the king, who has assigned your food and drink. Why should he see you looking worse than the other young men your age? The king would then have my head because of you."

Daniel then said to the guard whom the chief official had appointed over Daniel, Hananiah, Mishael and Azariah, "Please test your servants for ten days: Give us nothing but vegetables to eat and water to drink. Then compare our appearance with that of the young men who eat the royal food, and treat your servants in accordance with what you see." So he agreed to this and tested them for ten days.

Daniel 1:8–14

What beliefs had Daniel come to?	What choices did he have?	What evidence is there his belief had become a value?
_____	_____	_____
_____	_____	_____
_____	_____	_____
_____	_____	_____

ANALYSIS
continued.

So the administrators and the satraps went as a group to the king and said : "O King Darius, live forever! The royal administrators, prefects, satraps, advisers and governors have all agreed that the king should issue an edict and enforce the decree that anyone who prays to any god or man during the next thirty days, except to you, O king, shall be thrown into the lions' den. Now, O king, issue the decree and put it in writing so that it cannot be altered—in accordance with the laws of the Medes and Persians, which cannot be annulled." So King Darius put the decree in writing.

Now when Daniel learned that the decree had been published, he went home to his upstairs room where the windows opened toward Jerusalem. Three times a day he got down on his knees and prayed, giving thanks to his God, just as he had done before. Then these men went as a group and found Daniel praying and asking God for help.

Daniel 6:6–11

What beliefs had Daniel come to?

What choices did he have?

What evidence is there his belief had become a value?

_____

_____

_____

_____

_____

_____

_____

_____

_____

_____

_____

_____

Close this session with prayer.

INSIGHT

1 Look at the values listed on pages 8 and 9 as your parents'. How many were beliefs rather than true values? What does this tell you about your early experience with values?

_____

_____

_____

2 Look over the questions on pages 18–20. Which of the ones you strongly agreed with seem to you to be beliefs and which true values?

_____

_____

_____

3 Which items on pages 18–20 are in the *process* of becoming true values?

_____

_____

_____

_____

FREEDOM VS. CONTROL

Luke 15:11–32

Many people think of "values" in terms of the lists of do's and don'ts that some Christian communities have adopted. I reveal my values, they seem to think, by refusing to do this, or by insisting that I do that.

But when we look into Scripture, we begin to realize that value issues are far deeper; that values, those that are important to *God,* deal with the basics of our relationship with other people, ourselves, and our world. Our way of perceiving others and the situations we find ourselves in is intimately linked to our understanding of what is important to God—and thus a value that I will want to choose.

So let's begin looking into the Bible . . . and looking at values that Scripture teaches are important to God.

READ

Discovery at Wahweap

by Norm

I'd been anticipating this day for several months. Now I stood on the deck of the fifty-five-foot-long houseboat at Wahweap Marina on Lake Powell. The young man who was checking out the houseboat had only a few more words to say.

"You'll have to operate the houseboat around the Marina area so I can show you how to handle it. Then pull up to that dock, and the rest can bring their gear aboard."

I'd hardly grasped the wheel when the uneasiness began. This eleven-ton craft was hard to control! When I spun the wheel, it turned slowly and uncertainly. To slow it down I had to place the engines in reverse (without stalling) and accelerate. Even then the stubborn craft seemed reluctant to come to a stop.

I felt very uncomfortable . . . that things were out of control. To make matters worse, several of the interns I had been working with in local churches were watching me. I was pretty sure they weren't impressed by my leadership skills!

During the three day trip that followed I had to contend with that unresponsive houseboat . . . and my own feelings of frustration and uneasiness. But in the process, God helped me discover something very important about myself. *I was uneasy when I couldn't control!* I was particularly uncomfortable when I felt responsible. If someone else had been responsible for the houseboat, I'd have been up on the top deck happily sunbathing!

But now the Lord had my attention. And He began to apply the lesson. I realized that I tended to control my wife so I would feel more secure. I realized I did the same with my children. I wanted to be sure they would do the right things . . . and, usually, do them my way! I wanted them to be good children, without giving them the chance to choose the good for themselves. I controlled the circumstances so they *had* to go my way.

I've been very grateful for God's powerful lesson. It has made a real change in my life.

Now

Turn to the next page, and discuss in groups of eight the three questions recorded there. Jot down the insights and ideas of the group. Take up to twenty or twenty-five minutes.

DISCUSS

in your group
of eight.

Jot down
ideas and
insights your
group comes
up with.

1 What is *wrong* with a "controlling" approach in personal relationships? Why do people tend to take this approach?

_____

_____

_____

2 How do we try to control others? (How have you felt controlled? How have you tried to control?)

_____

_____

Time:
20–25 minutes

_____

3 Norm says his discovery made a real difference in his life. What changes would you expect to be made in his lifestyle?

_____

_____

_____

READ

One story told by Jesus is
clearly intended to mirror our
own relationship with God.
And reveal how God, as a good and
loving Father, relates to us.

Read the story individually.

There was a man who had two sons. The younger one said to his father, "Father, give me my share of the estate." So he divided his property between them.

Not long after that, the younger son got together all he had, set off for a distant country and there squandered his wealth in wild living. After he had spent everything, there was a severe famine in that whole country, and he began to be in need. So he went and hired himself out to a citizen of that country, who sent him to his fields to feed pigs. He longed to fill his stomach with the pods that the pigs were eating, but no one gave him anything.

When he came to his senses, he said, "How many of my father's hired men have food to spare, and here I am starving to death! I will set out and go back to my father and say to him: Father, I have sinned against heaven and against you. I am no longer worthy to be called your son; make me like one of your hired men." So he got up and went to his father.

But while he was still a long way off, his father saw him and was filled with compassion for him; he ran to his son, threw his arms around him and kissed him.

The son said to him, "Father, I have sinned against heaven and against you. I am no longer worthy to be called your son."

But the father said to his servants, "Quick! Bring the best robe and put it on him. Put a ring on his finger and sandals on his feet. Bring the fattened calf and kill it. Let's have a feast and celebrate. For this son of mine was dead and is alive again; he was lost and is found." So they began to celebrate.

Luke 15:11–24

How would you characterize the Father here:

___ Controlling   ___ Providing Freedom

Now, together, work through the story again guided by the process on the next pages.

Discuss

the statements made about
each segment of the story.

Demand for Freedom

There was a man who had two sons. The younger one said to his father, "Father, give me my share of the estate." So he divided his property between them.

Statements to discuss:

1 The young man demanded his freedom.

2 The father valued the son's freedom more than half his estate.

3 The father knew the risks of giving the son the property.

Freedom Misused

Not long after that, the younger son got together all he had, set off for a distant country and there squandered his wealth in wild living. After he had spent everything, there was a severe famine in that whole country, and he began to be in need. So he went and hired himself out to a citizen of that country, who sent him to his fields to feed pigs. He longed to fill his stomach with the pods that the pigs were eating, but no one gave him anything.

Statements to discuss:

1 There is always a risk in granting freedom.

2 Freedom misused leads to misery.

Freedom's Impact

When he came to his senses, he said, "How many of my father's hired men have food to spare, and here I am starving to death! I will set out and go back to my father and say to him: Father, I have sinned against heaven and against you. I am no longer worthy to be called your son; make me like one of your hired men." So he got up and went to his father.

Statements to discuss:

1 When we have freedom to choose, we become responsible for the consequences of our choices.

2 It was through the consequences that growth and change occurred.

Freedom's Outcome

While he was still a long way off, his father saw him and was filled with compassion for him; he ran to his son, threw his arms around him and kissed him.

The son said to him, "Father, I have sinned against heaven and against you. I am no longer worthy to be called your son."

But the father said to his servants, "Quick! Bring the best robe and put it on him. Put a ring on his finger and sandals on his feet. Bring the fattened calf and kill it. Let's have a feast and celebrate. For this son of mine was dead and is alive again; he was lost and is found." So they began to celebrate.

Statements to discuss:

1 Freedom abused does not destroy relationships.

2 The son had enough confidence in the father's love to return.

3 Wrong choices did not lead to recrimination; the right choices brought celebration.

Summary

Control keeps people from learning through their mistakes; freedom brings growth as the consequences of choices are experienced.

Control tends to put relationships on a performance basis; freedom keeps relationships on an unconditional love and grace basis.

Control reduces risk, but curtails growth; freedom increases risk, but does so in order to facilitate growth.

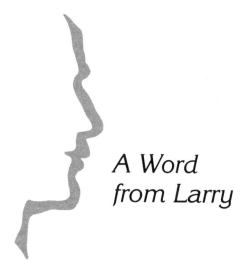

A Word
from Larry

Freedom is not Abandonment

God is the one who provides the perfect model of giving freedom. He does not control us, but He does make the implications for our choices clear to us. And he continues to communicate His deep love to us.

The relationship of committed love is God's kind of context for providing freedom. We may free a person we do not love—and this is, in effect, abandonment. It is a statement that we do not care enough to want to be involved.

For the Christian, however, a loving relationship is vital. We are to love others, as God has loved us (John 13:34). Where the assurance of that kind of love exists, we *can* risk the giving of freedom. And, as we give freedom, we can stay close and communicate our caring.

Perhaps you've experienced this love: a love that keeps on caring, yet resists controlling and extends a godly freedom. If so, you can thank God for such people in your lives. Even as those whom you love can thank God for you when you model Christ's approach to extending freedom.

CLOSE
this session
with prayer.

INSIGHT

1 Think again about your answers to these five freedom/control items which were on the questionnaire on pages 18–20.

On the left mark each item: SA (strongly agree), A (agree), ? (uncertain), D (disagree), SD (strongly disagree).

___ 1. We ought to protect others from making mistakes. ___
    (3.)
___ 2. A healthy individual should desire freedom. (8.)   ___
___ 3. When a person begins to fail, others should step in   ___
    and take over. (16.)
___ 4. Parents are responsible to be sure their children   ___
    make right choices. (23.)
___ 5. It is more important for parents to build a loving re-   ___
    lationship with children than to require obedience.
    (12.)

On the right, mark each item: C (characterizes the kind of person I am), B (describes the kind of person I am becoming), D (does not describe me).

2 Go to chapter two and compare your original answers. Are there any of the original answers you now feel uncomfortable with?

_____

_____

_____

_____

3 Write in the circles names of persons with whom you have significant relationships.

If in your relationship there is freedom granted *both ways* draw a dotted line between the circles. If freedom only one way, draw a solid line with an arrow to indicate it. How can you work to build freedom relationships in every case?

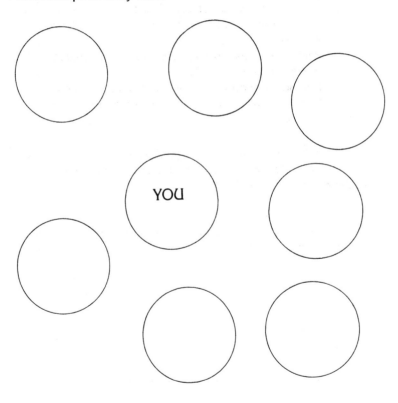

PEOPLE VS. POSSESIONS 5

Matthew 6:19-21; 25-33

There is nothing in Scripture to suggest that it's wrong to be wealthy. Or to have many possessions. What Scripture does say, clearly, is that "a man's life does not consist in the abundance of his possessions."

It's clear that there is danger—danger that our possessions might own us, rather than we own them!

There are vital value issues raised by material possessions. What should we spend our lives on? What is so valuable that we commit our time, our energy, and our thoughts to gain?

That is the question raised in this week's exploration of God's values. That's the question each of us will want to ask in exploring our values.

Discuss

"There was a man who had two sons. The younger one said to his father, 'Father, give me my share of the estate.'"

1 Which would be harder for most people: To give a child freedom? To give up much of one's estate?

2 Why?

CIRCLE

What feelings do you associate with:

having plenty of money?	not having much money?
SECURITY	ANXIETY
POWER	RESENTMENT
COMFORT	SHAME
PLEASURE	ENVY
STATUS	RESTRICTION
PRIDE	SELF-RIGHTEOUSNESS
FREEDOM	POWERLESSNESS
SIGNIFICANCE	INSIGNIFICANCE
CONTROL	FUTILITY

SHARE

In groups of eight share an
incident or two when you
experienced one of the feelings
you circled.

DEBATE

Within your group of eight,
debate the following proposition
for five or six minutes,
half taking the negative side
and half taking the affirmative side.

RESOLVED: None of these feelings are
really related to money:

SECURITY	ANXIETY
POWER	RESENTMENT
COMFORT	SHAME
PLEASURE	ENVY
STATUS	RESTRICTION
PRIDE	SELF-RIGHTEOUSNESS
FREEDOM	POWERLESSNESS
SIGNIFICANCE	INSIGNIFICANCE
CONTROL	FUTILITY

STUDY
this passage from
Matthew individually.

Therefore I tell you, do not worry about your life, what you will eat or drink; or about your body, what you will wear. Is not life more important than food, and the body more important than clothes? Look at the birds of the air; they do not sow or reap or store away in barns, and yet your heavenly Father feeds them. Are you not much more valuable than they? Who of you by worrying can add a single hour to his life?

And why do you worry about clothes? See how the lilies of the field grow. They do not labor or spin. Yet I tell you that not even Solomon in all his splendor was dressed like one of these. If that is how God clothes the grass of the field, which is here today and tomorrow is thrown into the fire, will he not much more clothe you, O you of little faith? So do not worry, saying, "What shall we eat?" or "What shall we drink?" or "What shall we wear?" For the pagans run after all these things, and your heavenly Father knows that you need them. But seek first his kingdom and his righteousness, and all these things will be given to you as well.

Matthew 6:25–34

WRITE

in the target what you believe to be the main teaching of this passage.

FILL IN TOGETHER

What does each verse suggest
about the wisdom of these views?
Write down your ideas.

Matthew gives us these points of view on money.	You cannot serve God and money. *Matthew 6:24*
God's view "I will supply (money) for My children to meet their needs."	
General view "Must concentrate on gaining (money) if I am to be secure and significant."	
Believer's view "Because I know I am significant to God, I trust Him to meet my needs, and I am free to (stop worrying about money and) care about others."	

Do not store up for yourselves treasures on earth, where moth and rust destroy, and where thieves break in and steal. But store up for yourselves treasures in heaven, where moth and rust do not destroy, nor thieves break through and steal. *Matthew 6:19–20*	Where your treasure is, there will your heart be also. *Matthew 6:21*

	Do not worry about tomorrow, for tomorrow will worry about itself. *Matthew 6:34*	Godliness with contentment is great gain. *1 Timothy 6:6*
God's view		
General view		
Believer's view		

The love of money is a root of all kinds of evil. Some people, eager for money, have wandered from the faith and pierced themselves with many griefs. *1 Timothy 6:10*	Command those who are rich in this present world not to be arrogant or put their hope in wealth . . . to do good, to be rich in good deeds, and to be generous and willing to share. *1 Timothy 6:17–18*

Summary

Significance and confidence are not rooted in our possessions but in the fact that we are important to God. He places supreme value on *persons* . . . never on things. When we adopt His values, we are freed *from* the nagging demand that we focus our lives on gaining wealth . . . and freed *to* focus our lives on what God Himself sees as primary values: loving and serving others, and thus seeking to live as members of His kingdom.

Together

Look over the list of words describing feelings associated with either having plenty of money or not having much money. Which of them do you feel can be crossed off the lists as not actually being related to possessions, as far as Christian experience is concerned? Have reasons for each one you eliminate.

Having plenty of money?

Not having much money?

Having plenty of money?	Not having much money?
SECURITY	ANXIETY
POWER	RESENTMENT
COMFORT	SHAME
PLEASURE	ENVY
STATUS	RESTRICTION
PRIDE	SELF-RIGHTEOUSNESS
FREEDOM	POWERLESSNESS
SIGNIFICANCE	INSIGNIFICANCE
CONTROL	FUTILITY

Pray

Share any prayer requests with others, and pray together.

INSIGHT

1 Think again about your answers to these five people/possessions items which were on the questionnaire on pages 18–20.

On the left, mark each item: SA (strongly agree), A (agree), ? (uncertain), D (disagree), SD (strongly disagree).

___ 1. God wants His children to prosper financially. (28.) ___
___ 2. A Christian must always give priority to the financial security of his family. (34.) ___
___ 3. It is better to be wealthy than poor. (38.) ___
___ 4. Our use of money shows what is important to us. (5.) ___
___ 5. In our society, wealth is a valid way to measure importance. (18.) ___

On the right, mark each item: C (characterizes the kind of person I am), B (describes the kind of person I am becoming), D (does not describe me).

2 Review your last year's income tax returns. What do they show about your use and attitude toward money?

_____

_____

_____

_____

_____

_____

3 Place check marks on the "balance" side where you have tended to place greatest emphasis this past year.

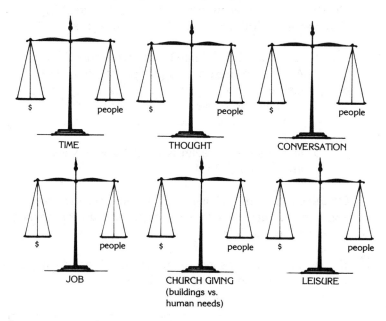

4 State a meaningful goal for your growth in this area.

_____

_____

_____

_____

PERSONAL GROWTH VS. CONFORMITY ①

Matthew 10:1–10

The Bible draws a contrast between transformation
and conformity. It describes conformity as
being "squeezed into the world's mold" (Romans 12:1).

We all want to be transformed. But we do not always
value or welcome the situation in which we grow beyond conformity.

In this session we will explore together something which God
values very highly, and something which we too often try to avoid.

WRITE

In the box indicate
one area in your
life where you feel
strong pressures to
conform.

Label the arrows
to show the kinds of
pressures you feel
in this area.

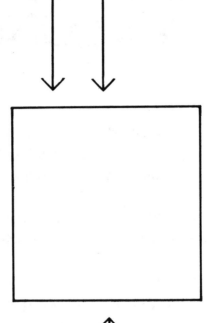

SHARE

In groups of eight
share the areas
and the pressures
from page 70.

INDIVIDUALLY

Underline phrases that indicate pressures on the disciples in the new situation (e.g., the statement "Do not take along gold or silver or copper" equals financial pressures). Watch for both internal and external pressures. Identify the pressure that you have underlined in the margin. We've done the first two for you.

He called his twelve disciples to him and <u>gave them authority</u> to drive out evil spirits and to cure every kind of disease and sickness.   ← *pressure of responsibility*

These twelve Jesus sent out with the following instructions: "Do not go among the Gentiles or enter any town of the Samaritans. Go rather to the lost sheep of Israel. As you go, preach this message: 'The kingdom of heaven is near.' Heal the sick, raise the dead, cleanse those who have leprosy, drive out demons. Freely you have received, freely give. <u>Do not take along any gold or silver or copper in your belts</u>; take no bag for the journey, or extra tunic, or sandals or a staff; for the worker is worth his keep.   ← *financial pressure*

"Whatever town or village you enter, search for some worthy person there and stay at his house until you leave. As you enter the home, give it your greeting. If the home is deserving, let your peace rest on it; if it is not, let your peace return to you. If anyone will not welcome you or listen to your words, shake the dust off your feet when you leave that home or town. I tell you the truth, it will be more bearable for Sodom and Gomorrah on the day of judgment than for that town.

"I am sending you out like sheep among wolves. Therefore be as shrewd as snakes and as innocent as doves. But be on your guard against men; they will hand you over to the local councils and flog you in their synagogues. On my account you will be brought before governors and kings as witnesses to them and to the Gentiles. But when they arrest you, do not worry about what to say or how to say it. At that time you will be given what to say, for it will not be you speaking, but the Spirit of your Father speaking through you.

"Brother will betray brother to death, and a father his child; children will rebel against their parents and have them put to death. All men will hate you because of me, but he who stands firm to the end will be saved. When you are persecuted in one place, flee to another. I tell you the truth, you will not finish going through the cities of Israel before the Son of Man comes.

"A student is not above his teacher, nor a servant above his master. It is enough for the student to be like his teacher, and the servant like his master. If the head of the house has been called Beelzebub, how much more the members of his household!

"So do not be afraid of them. There is nothing concealed that will not be disclosed, or hidden that will not be made known. What I tell you in the dark, speak in the daylight; what is whispered in your ear, proclaim from the housetops. Do not be afraid of those who kill the body but cannot kill the soul. Rather, be afraid of the one who can destroy both soul and body in hell. Are not two sparrows sold for a penny? Yet not one of them will fall to the ground apart from the will of your Father. And even the very hairs of your head are all numbered. So don't be afraid; you are worth more than many sparrows.

"Anyone who loves his father or mother more than me is not worthy of me; anyone who loves his son or daughter more than me is not worthy of me; and anyone who does not take his cross and follow me is not worthy of me. Whoever finds his life will lose it, and whoever loses his life for my sake will find it.

"He who receives you receives me, and he who receives me receives the one who sent me. Anyone who receives a prophet because he is a prophet will receive a prophet's reward, and anyone who receives a righteous man because he is a righteous man will receive a righteous man's reward. And if anyone gives a cup of cold water to one of these little ones because he is my disciple, I tell you the truth, he will certainly not lose his reward."

Matthew 10:1, 5–30, 37–42

DISCUSS
the pressures you discovered. Which are internal? Which external? Which do you feel would be hardest to resist?

risk

Few of us like the pressures that squeeze us to conform. But all of us realize there is always risk involved in breaking out of the boxes in which our lives are compressed. And also we realize that living under pressure can be one way God works to mature us.

But *risk* is also a pathway God uses to move us toward personal growth. God does not hesitate to put us in situations which are new to us . . . which stretch us and give us opportunities to grow.

God has never placed great value on conforming for the sake of security! Instead Jesus' whole life with His disciples shows that He was constantly stretching them; constantly exposing them to opportunities for growth that, at the same time, did involve risk.

You've looked at Matthew 10 and identified the pressures (and thus the risks) faced by the disciples. On the next pages *underline the same phrases.* But now, along the side, identify the opportunity for growth that risking that pressure provided.

He called his twelve disciples to him and <u>gave them authority</u> to drive out evil spirits and to cure every kind of disease and sickness.

opportunity to be responsible ←

These twelve Jesus sent out with the following instructions: "Do not go among the Gentiles or enter any town of the Samaritans. Go rather to the lost sheep of Israel. As you go, preach this message: 'The kingdom of heaven is near.' Heal the sick, raise the dead, cleanse those who have leprosy, drive out demons. Freely you have received, freely give. <u>Do not take along any gold or silver or copper in your belts</u>; take no bag for the journey, or extra tunic, or sandals or a staff; for the worker is worth his keep.

reason to trust God ←

"Whatever town or village you enter, search for some worthy person there and stay at his house until you leave. As you enter the home, give it your greeting. If the home is deserving, let your peace rest on it; if it is not, let your peace return to you. If anyone will not welcome you or listen to your words, shake the dust off your feet when you leave that home or town. I tell you the truth, it will be more bearable for Sodom and Gomorrah on the day of judgment than for that town.

"I am sending you out like sheep among wolves. Therefore be as shrewd as snakes and as innocent as doves. But be on your guard against men; they will hand you over to the local councils and flog you in their synagogues. On my account you will be brought before governors and kings as witnesses to them and to the Gentiles. But when they arrest you, do not worry about what to say or how to say it. At that time you will be given what to say, for it will not be you speaking, but the Spirit of your Father speaking through you.

"Brother will betray brother to death, and a father his child; children will rebel against their parents and have them put to death. All men will hate you because of me, but he who stands firm to the end will be saved. When you are persecuted in one place, flee to another. I tell you the truth, you will not finish going through the cities of Israel before the Son of Man comes.

"A student is not above his teacher, nor a servant above his master. It is enough for the student to be like his teacher, and the servant like his master. If the head of the house has been called Beelzebub, how much more the members of his household!

"So do not be afraid of them. There is nothing concealed that will not be disclosed, or hidden that will not be made known. What I tell you in the dark, speak in the daylight; what is whispered in your ear, proclaim from the house-tops. Do not be afraid of those who kill the body but cannot kill the soul. Rather, be afraid of the one who can destroy both soul and body in hell. Are not two sparrows sold for a penny? Yet not one of them will fall to the ground apart from the will of your Father. And even the very hairs of your head are all numbered. So don't be afraid; you are worth more than many sparrows.

"Anyone who loves his father or mother more than me is not worthy of me; anyone who loves his son or daughter more than me is not worthy of me; and anyone who does not take his cross and follow me is not worthy of me. Whoever finds his life will lose it, and whoever loses his life for my sake will find it.

"He who receives you receives me, and he who receives me receives the one who sent me. Anyone who receives a prophet because he is a prophet will receive a prophet's reward, and anyone who receives a righteous man because he is a righteous man will receive a righteous man's reward. And if anyone gives a cup of cold water to one of these little ones because he is my disciple, I tell you the truth, he will certainly not lose his reward."

Matthew 10:1, 5–30, 37–42

DISCUSS
together the "opportunities."

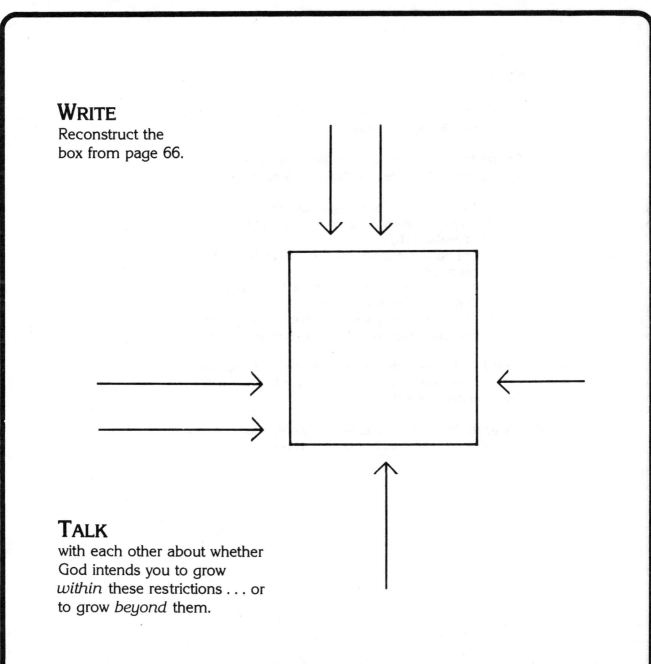

WRITE
Reconstruct the
box from page 66.

TALK
with each other about whether
God intends you to grow
within these restrictions . . . or
to grow *beyond* them.

INSIGHT

1 Think again about your answers to these five conformity/personal growth items from pages 18–20.

On the left mark each item: SA (strongly agree), A (agree), ? (uncertain), D (disagree), SD (strongly disagree).

___ 1. A person should be willing to take risks. (29.)   ___
___ 2. People who learn to live within their limitations are   ___
        admirable. (31.)
___ 3. One ought not to tackle more than he is sure he   ___
        can handle. (40.)
___ 4. If a person is not growing he is falling short of   ___
        God's intention for him. (9.)
___ 5. There are some opportunities that are too great to   ___
        miss out on, no matter how old a person is. (13.)

On the right, mark each item: C (characterizes the kind of person I am), B (describes the kind of person I am becoming), D (does not describe me).

2 Reread the Matthew 10 passage daily and ask God to help you *see* your own unique opportunities for growth.

SUCCESS VS. "SUCCESS" 7

Luke 12:16–21; 16:19–25

The concept of "success" is often a cloudy
one. There's not only room for achievement
in Christian experience: there is encouragement
in Christ to be and to do our best.

Actually, the real issue we all face is this.
What *is* "success"? Does our view
of achievement reflect God's values,
or something different?

INDIVIDUALLY

Jot down here incidents when
you experienced success.

My successes as a child	My successes as a teen

My successes as a young adult	My successes since age 26
_____	_____
_____	_____
_____	_____
_____	_____
_____	_____
_____	_____
_____	_____
_____	_____
_____	_____
_____	_____
_____	_____

SHARE

in groups of five or six
the successes you listed on
pages 76 and 77.

As each person shares,
write down "what success is"
to him or her.

Success is . . .

FOR _____
(name)

_____

_____

FOR _____
(name)

_____

_____

FOR _____
(name)

_____

_____

FOR _____
(name)

_____

_____

FOR _____
(name)

_____

_____

FOR _____
(name)

_____

TELL

Have the rest of the group
tell each person what
they perceived as
his or her definition
of success.

Jot down the others' definitions
of "success" for you.

_____

_____

_____

_____

_____

DIVIDE

into two study groups.
Each analyze one Bible passage
and determine *what success was*
to the individual described.
(Spend about ten minutes.)

The ground of a certain rich man produced a good crop. He thought to himself "What shall I do? I have no place to store my crops."

Then he said, "This is what I'll do. I will tear down my barns and build bigger ones, and there I will store all my grain and my goods. And I'll say to myself, 'You have plenty of good things laid up for many years. Take life easy; eat, drink and be merry.'"

But God said to him, "You fool! This very night your life will be demanded from you. Then who will get what you have prepared for yourself?"

This is how it will be with anyone who stores up things for himself but is not rich toward God.

Luke 12:16–21

Success to this man was:

_____

_____

_____

_____

There was a rich man who was dressed in purple and fine linen and lived in luxury every day. At his gate was laid a beggar named Lazarus, covered with sores and longing to eat what fell from the rich man's table. Even the dogs came and licked his sores.

The time came when the beggar died and the angels carried him to Abraham's side. The rich man also died and was buried. In hell, where he was in torment, he looked up and saw Abraham far away, with Lazarus by his side. So he called to him, "Father Abraham, have pity on me and send Lazarus to dip the tip of his finger in water and cool my tongue, because I am in agony in this fire."

But Abraham replied, "Son, remember that in your lifetime you received your good things, while Lazarus received bad things, but now he is comforted here and you are in agony."

Luke 16:19–25

Success to this man was:

_____

_____

_____

_____

SHARE

together what each group saw
as the success profile of
the individual they studied.

1 What did the man in Luke 12 overlook in his drive for success?

_____

_____

2 What did the man in Luke 16 overlook in his drive for success?

_____

_____

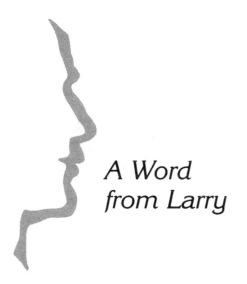

A Word from Larry

Success

Jesus spoke about the person who gained the whole world, but who lost himself in that process. This is the kind of person portrayed in Luke 12. He felt that his life consisted in the things that he possessed and failed to develop himself or his relationship with God.

Jesus also spoke of persons like the man portrayed in Luke 16. Though some even called Him, "Lord, Lord," Jesus turned them away. Their unconcern for the stranger, the naked, the hungry, and the thirsty and imprisoned, revealed fully that their hearts had never been touched by Jesus' love.

Jesus Himself is our most perfect example of God's view of success. He was rejected. Persecuted. Despised. Yet through it all He maintained His commitment to obey the Father. And through it all He set aside His own needs to give Himself for others. Out of that life of love and commitment flowed the salvation we all enjoy . . . and glory that we shall share.

The externals were never good measures of success. They did not indicate reality in the case of the men of Luke 12 and 16. They did not indicate reality in the case of our Lord. Where there is commitment to God's will and commitment to a deep and caring concern for others there will always be success in God's eyes. And it is His view that counts.

20 YEARS LATER

Looking back twenty years from
now, I would like the pattern
of my life to reveal that
success to me **was**

_____

_____

_____

SHARE
your definitions
(above) and close in
prayer.

INSIGHT

1 Think again about your answers to these five success/"success" items from pages 18–20.

On the left, mark each item: SA (strongly agree), A (agree), ? (uncertain), D (disagree), SD (strongly disagree).

___ 1. A person needs a college education to be a success in life. (22.) ___

___ 2. One ought to measure "success" by growth in self and others. (2.) ___

___ 3. Normally God will give faithful believers material blessings. (27.) ___

___ 4. It is wrong to want to be a success on earth. (7.) ___

___ 5. The accomplishments that give us the greatest pleasure indicate our view of success. (17.) ___

On the right, mark each item: C (characterizes the kind of person I am), B (describes the kind of person I am becoming), D (does not describe me).

2 Read daily in Ecclesiastes this week. What did the writer discover about "success"?

Day 1.   Ecclesiastes 1:12–18
Day 2.   Ecclesiastes 2:1–11
Day 3.   Ecclesiastes 2:17–26
Day 4.   Ecclesiastes 5:8–12
Day 5.   Ecclesiastes 6:1–11
Day 6.   Ecclesiastes 12:1–10

3 Think again about your life over the past five years. Make a list here of your "successes" from God's point of view.

_____

_____

_____

_____

_____

_____

WORK AND LEISURE 8

Luke 10:38–41

In the last four sessions we looked at values in conflict. We saw values that were wrong or inadequate *contrasted* with biblical values which reflect a very different, divine perspective on life.

In the next four studies—including this one—we are going to explore values that must be kept in balance. Both work and enjoyment of God's good gifts are seen in Scripture as good. But neither is to be chosen at the expense of the other.

There are many such values that keep us in a kind of tension as we struggle to balance them in our lives. In these areas there is no clear-cut "right" or "wrong" pattern. But there is a need to see each contrasting value from God's perspective. And let Him guide us to His balance of these values in our lives.

CHECK
each statement
that describes you.

___ I can't wait to get off work and go home.
___ My identity is tied up with my work.
___ I have many interests which occupy my time.
___ I'd rather read than mow the lawn.
___ I feel guilty if I'm not working.
___ I'm often tempted to treat my "sick days" like vacation time.
___ I plan my leisure time as carefully as I do my work.
___ People would call me a workaholic.
___ I regularly make time for relaxation.
___ My reading is almost all related to my work.
___ Work has been so unsatisfying that I' change jobs frequently.
___ I work hard at being a Christian.
___ It's more important to me to have fun times with my children than serve on the church board.
___ I insist that my children excel in school.
___ It's very hard for me to relax without wanting to do something.
___ I enjoy having friends over for relaxed times together.
___ Our church calendar keeps me busy.
___ I've enjoyed playing with my children since they were very young.
___ My wife and I regularly enjoy times out together.
___ I have no hobbies.
___ People at church make me feel guilty if I'm not actively serving.

___ Work often keeps me from getting enough sleep.
___ Our family frequently goes on outings.
___ I feel my spouse neglects me because of work.
___ Life is basically boring.
___ The TV is almost always on in our house.
___ I tend to be a perfectionist in my work.
___ It's not unusual for us to take our children out of school for some other enriching experience.
___ I have difficulty knowing how to use my leisure time.
___ I am basically lazy.
___ If I didn't have to work, I wouldn't.
___ I fear retirement.
___ To me, work is really fun.
___ I work more hours a week than most people.
___ I work more than I should to provide extras for my family.
___ Family or personal vacations are the high point of my year.
___ I work hard now so I'll be secure and able to relax when I retire.
___ I enjoy many fun activities at our church.
___ I am basically a relaxed person.
___ I work a lot of overtime.
___ I could be described as a "fulfilled" individual.
___ My spouse encourages me to enrich my leisure time.
___ Much of my reading focuses on hobbies and other interests.

WRITE
from the items
you chose

the three
statements that
are *most true*
of me.

1 _____
_____

2 _____
_____

3 _____
_____

the three
statements that
are *least true*
of me.

1 _____
_____

2 _____
_____

3 _____
_____

SHARE

the "most true"
and "least true" statements
in your group of eight.

READ ALOUD

The central question remains: what is the meaning and purpose of life? If we, as Christians, do not demonstrate as well as speak a different reply than the world around us, then where is our message? If we try to rationalize our compulsive work habits by saying we are accomplishing things for God, then logically we aren't *anything* unless we are *doing* something. To make matters worse, we have taken these workaholic habits beyond the realm of work to include our personal, social, and spiritual lives as well. In our attempts to make our deeper commitments more "useful," we slowly become mere functionaries. Our prayer life becomes only a time to ask God to do things for us so that we can be better workers for Him. The purpose and privilege of simply knowing Him and enjoying Him forever is considered unproductive. Our marriages slide quietly into what we can do for each other—the husband becoming a lawn mower and garbage remover, and the wife only keeping the house clean and the kids quiet. Children's usefulness is unclear, and in a culture infatuated with practicality, kids begin to see themselves as worthless. Friends are recognized as opportunities, and therefore a justifiable expenditure of time. And religion becomes a pattern of rules and regulations, a system that helps us tidy up our behavior, somewhat like rearranging the deck chairs on the Titanic. It allows us a better view as we go down.[1]

[1]Tim Hansel, *When I Relax I Feel Guilty.* (Elgin, Illinois: David C. Cook, 1979), pp. 37–38.

Discuss
together

1 How satisfied am I with my own attitude toward and view of work?

2 In what ways are work and leisure in balance in my life? In what ways are they out of balance?

3 Does my church support a healthy balance between work and leisure in its members' lives or does it undermine a balance?

WRITE

your own commentary
on this passage.
Be sure to note
the choices involved,
the emotional states revealed,
and the consequences
of the choices.

As Jesus and his disciples were on their way, he came to a village where a woman named Martha opened her home to him. She had a sister called Mary, who sat at the Lord's feet listening to what he said. But Martha was distracted by all the preparations that had to be made. She came to him and asked, "Lord, don't you care that my sister has left me to do the work by myself? Tell her to help me!"

"Martha, Martha," the Lord answered, "you are worried and upset about many things, but only one thing is needed. Mary has chosen what is better, and it will not be taken away from her."

Luke 10:38–41

_____

_____

_____

SHARE
your commentaries
with each other.

TOGETHER

agree on a statement
summing up Christ's perspective
on work and leisure.

Christ's Perspective on Work and Leisure

_____

_____

_____

_____

_____

_____

_____

INSIGHT

1 Think again about your answers to these five work/leisure items from pages 18–20.

On the left, mark each item: SA (strongly agree), A (agree), ? (uncertain), D (disagree), SD (strongly disagree).

___ 1. Work should have greater significance in life than ___
      leisure. (11.)
___ 2. Having hobbies is nice but unimportant. (25.) ___
___ 3. One should work hard to provide his or her family ___
      with extras. (33.)
___ 4. People who relax easily are probably lazy. (39.) ___
___ 5. Playing with children is a family priority. (4.) ___

On the right, mark each item: C (characterizes the kind of person I am), B (describes the kind of person I am becoming), D (does not describe me).

2 For meditation: This week prayerfully consider these quotes.

Quote 1 "Most middle-class Americans tend to worship their work, to work at their play, and to play at their worship. As a result, their meanings and values are distorted. Their relationships disintegrate faster than they can keep them in repair, and their life-styles resemble a cast of characters in search of a plot" (Gordon Dahl).[2]

[2]Hansel, *When I Relax,* p. 33.

Quote 2 "How do we break the spell and accept the invitation to a freer life-style? The first step is by letting go of the attitudes that would have us continually deny our health and happiness in an effort to be responsible. Let go of the fears of inconvenience. Let go of the need to constantly compare. Let go of some of the warm, comfortable, colorless, tasteless, abstract images you have of leisure, and leap out of some of your routines. Begin to refresh yourself in some of the simple joys of being alive. Turn off your TV for a while and experience again the thrill of living your life directly rather than vicariously, without all the baggage and parachutes."[3]

[3]Ibid., p. 44.

3 Each day this week jot down in the evening the amounts of time you committed to "work activities" and to "leisure." Are you satisfied this involves a healthy balance for you?

_____   _____

_____   _____

_____   _____

_____   _____

_____   _____

FAIRNESS AND GRACE

Matthew 20:1–15

One of the most difficult tensions we have
to keep in balance in our relationships with others
is that between fairness and grace.
We know it is right for persons to be responsible
for their actions—and make their own way in life.
How then do we both encourage responsibility
and encourage that element of graciousness
in relationships with others that is godly?
This is our focus for this session.

READ

this passage
carefully.

The kingdom of heaven is like a landowner who went out early in the morning to hire men to work in his vineyard. He agreed to pay them a denarius for the day and sent them into his vineyard.

About the third hour he went out and saw others standing in the marketplace doing nothing. He told them, "You also go and work in my vineyard, and I will pay you whatever is right." So they went.

He went out again about the sixth hour and the ninth hour and did the same thing. About the eleventh hour he went out and found still others standing around. He asked them, "Why have you been standing here all day long doing nothing?"

"Because no one has hired us," they answered.

He said to them, "You also go and work in my vineyard."

When evening came, the owner of the vineyard said to his foreman, "Call the workers and pay them their wages, beginning with the last ones hired and going on to the first."

The workers who were hired about the eleventh hour came and each received a denarius. So when those came who were hired first, they expected to receive more. But each of them also received a denarius. When they received it, they began to grumble against the landowner. "These men who were hired last worked only one hour," they said, "and you have made them equal to us who have borne the burden of the work and the heat of the day."

But he answered one of them, "Friend, I am not being unfair to you. Didn't you agree to work for a denarius? Take your pay and go. I want to give the man who was hired last the same as I gave you. Don't I have the right to do what I want with my own money? Or are you envious because I am generous?"

Matthew 20:1–15

IDENTIFY

with *one* of the
following story characters
and jot down your impressions
of his feelings, thoughts, attitudes.

1 The owner

2 A day-long worker

3 A partial-day worker

_____

_____

_____

_____

_____

_____

ROLE PLAY

Now take the role
of the individual
you identified with.
Discuss the incident
for ten minutes,
representing your
character's thoughts
and feelings.

READ

the underlined portions of the Bible study.

The kingdom of heaven is like a landowner who went out early in the morning to hire men to work in his vineyard. *He agreed to pay them a denarius for the day and sent them into his vineyard.*

About the third hour he went out and saw others standing in the marketplace doing nothing. He told them, "You also go and work in my vineyard, and I will pay you whatever is right." So they went.

He went out again about the sixth hour and the ninth hour and did the same thing. About the eleventh hour he went out and found still others standing around. He asked them, "Why have you been standing there all day long doing nothing?"

"Because no one has hired us," they answered.

He said to them, "You also go and work in my vineyard."

When evening came, the owner of the vineyard said to his foreman, "Call the workers and pay them their wages, beginning with the last ones hired and going on to the first."

The workers who were hired about the eleventh hour came and each received a denarius. *So when those came who were hired first, they expected to receive more. But each one of them also received a denarius. When they received it, they began to grumble against the landowner.* "These men who were hired last worked only one hour," they said, "and you have made them equal to us, who have borne the burden of the work and the heat of the day."

But he answered one of them, "Friend, I am not being unfair to you. Didn't you agree to work for a denarius? Take your pay and go. I want to give the man who was hired last the same as I gave you. Don't I have the right to do what I want with my own money? Or are you envious because I am generous?"

Then read issue #1 . . . and apply.

ISSUE #1

The landowner was completely fair in every aspect of his relationship with the full-day workers. He had made a contract with them, providing them with a full day's wages. He kept the contract to the letter. There was not even any performance criteria, for instance, "minimum 8 bushels plucked," built in! The people who wanted a change in the contract—who demanded it—were the workers.

What ways can you think of that a Christian can learn from—and apply—this truth in his personal relationship with God and others? Work together, and jot down application ideas.

_____

_____

_____

_____

_____

_____

_____

_____

READ

the underlined portions
of the Bible study.

The kingdom of heaven is like a landowner who went out early in the morning to hire men to work in his vineyard. *He agreed to pay them a denarius for the day and sent them into his vineyard.*

About the third hour he went out and saw others standing in the marketplace doing nothing. He told them, "You also go and work in my vineyard, and I will pay you whatever is right." So they went.

He went out again about the sixth hour and the ninth hour and did the same thing. About the eleventh hour he went out and found still others standing around. He asked them "Why have you been standing here all day long doing nothing?"

"Because no one has hired us," they answered.

He said to them, "You also go and work in my vineyard."

When evening came, the owner of the vineyard said to his foreman, "Call the workers and pay them their wages, beginning with the last ones hired and going on to the first."

The workers who were hired about the eleventh hour came and each received a denarius. So when those came who were hired first, they expected to receive more. But each one of them also received a denarius. When they received it, they began to grumble against the landowner. "These men who were hired last worked only one hour," they said, "and you have made them equal to us who have borne the burden of the work and the heat of the day."

But he answered one of them, "Friend, I am not being unfair to you. Didn't you agree to work for a denarius? Take your pay and go. I want to give the man who was hired last the same as I gave you. Don't I have the right to do what I want with my own money? Or are you envious because I am generous?"

Then read issue #2 . . . and apply.

ISSUE #2

The fair contract made with the full-day workers met their daily need. And the amount given to the workers who only served part of a day was also a "daily need" portion. The owner did not give them "something for nothing"—for each did work. And the owner did not give beyond the daily need of each. What the story shows is that either through fairness or a graciousness that went beyond fairness, the owner acted to meet the daily need of individuals he cared about as persons.

What ways can you think of that a Christian can learn from—and apply—this truth in his personal relationship with God and others? Work together, and jot down application ideas.

_____

_____

_____

_____

_____

_____

_____

READ
the underlined portions
of the Bible study.

The kingdom of heaven is like a landowner who went out early in the morning to hire men to work in his vineyard. He agreed to pay them a denarius for the day and sent them into his vineyard.

About the third hour he went out and saw others standing in the marketplace doing nothing. He told them, "You also go and work in my vineyard, and I will pay you whatever is right." So they went.

He went out again about the sixth hour and the ninth hour and did the same thing. About the eleventh hour he went out and found still others standing around. He asked them "Why have you been standing here all day long doing nothing?"

"Because no one has hired us," they answered.

He said to them, "You also go and work in my vineyard."

When evening came, the owner of the vineyard said to his foreman, "Call the workers and pay them their wages, beginning with the last ones hired and going on to the first."

The workers who were hired about the eleventh hour came and each received a denarius. So when those came who were hired first, they expected to receive more. But each one of them also received a denarius. When they received it, they began to grumble against the landowner. *"These men who were hired last worked only one hour," they said, "and you have made them equal to us who have borne the burden of the work and the heat of the day."*

But he answered one of them, "Friend, I am not being unfair to you. Didn't you agree to work for a denarius? *Take your pay and go. I want to give the man who was hired last the same as I gave you. Don't I have the right to do what I want with my own money? Or are you envious because I am generous?"*

Then read issue #3 . . . and apply.

ISSUE #3

The action of the owner flowed from his own generosity. The source of his action was not a response to what others had done, but rather was a response to his own generous nature. While we want to protect the right to fair treatment, isn't it also important to protect the right of others to be generous with what is theirs?

What ways can you think of that a Christian can learn from—and apply—this truth in his personal relationship with God and others? Work together, and jot down application ideas.

_____

_____

_____

_____

_____

_____

_____

_____

_____

_____

READ

the underlined portions
of the Bible study.

The kingdom of heaven is like a landowner who went out early in the morning to hire men to work in his vineyard. He agreed to pay them a denarius for the day and sent them into his vineyard.

About the third hour he went out and saw others standing in the marketplace doing nothing. He told them, "You also go and work in my vineyard, and I will pay you whatever is right." So they went.

He went out again about the sixth hour and the ninth hour and did the same thing. About the eleventh hour he went out and found still others standing around. He asked them "Why have you been standing here all day long doing nothing?"

"Because no one has hired us," they answered.

He said to them, "You also go and work in my vineyard."

When evening came, the owner of the vineyard said to his foreman, "Call the workers and pay them their wages, beginning with the last ones hired and going on to the first."

The workers who were hired about the eleventh hour came and each received a denarius. So when those came who were hired first, they expected to receive more. But each one of them also received a denarius. _When they received it, they began to grumble against the landowner. "These men who were hired last worked only one hour," they said, "and you have made them equal to us who have borne the burden of the work and the heat of the day."_

But he answered one of them, "Friend, I am not being unfair to you. Didn't you agree to work for a denarius? Take your pay and go. I want to give the man who was hired last the same as I gave you. Don't I have the right to do what I want with my own money? Or are you envious because I am generous?"

Then read issue #4 . . . and apply.

ISSUE #4

The reaction of the full-day workers is striking. They grumbled, the passage says. And it suggests that they were envious of the others. How do we react when other people are the recipients of obvious grace? Do we rejoice when we see God meet their needs in a unique way and forget that, although He may choose another means, He has also met ours? God does make us all equal: He cares for all of us, though the means through which His care is expressed will differ.

What ways can you think of that a Christian can learn from—and apply—this truth in his personal relationship with God and others? Work together, and jot down application ideas.

_____

_____

_____

_____

_____

_____

_____

_____

INSIGHT

1 Think again about your answers to these five fairness/grace items from pages 18–20.

On the left, mark each item: SA (strongly agree), A (agree), ? (uncertain), D (disagree), SD (strongly disagree).

___ 1. It's only right to work for what we get in life. (36.)   ___
___ 2. It is demeaning to accept charity. (6.)   ___
___ 3. We should teach our children to pull their own   ___
      weight. (24.)
___ 4. We have a right to be generous with others instead   ___
      of being merely fair. (15.)
___ 5. We ought to treat all others equally and fairly. (20.)   ___

On the right, mark each item: C (characterizes the kind of person I am), B (describes the kind of person I am becoming), D (does not describe me).

2 During the week meditate daily on your own relationship with God. Are you letting both His fairness and grace have their way in you?

SERVING AND SERVED

John 13:1–17

Jesus found great joy in
serving others.
And He invites us
to a servant lifestyle.

But there is more
to servanthood than
most of us
realize.

Servanthood Means Touching

EACH PERSON

Take something from
your wallet or purse
that a person in your
group may need, and
give it to him or her.

SHARE
with each other how
you felt in this experience.

TOGETHER
read this passage.

The evening meal was being served, and the devil had already prompted Judas Iscariot, son of Simon, to betray Jesus. Jesus knew that the Father had put all things under his power, and that he had come from God and was returning to God; so he got up from the meal, took off his outer clothing, and wrapped a towel around his waist. After that, he poured water into a basin and began to wash his disciples' feet, drying them with the towel that was wrapped around him.

He came to Simon Peter, who said to him, "Lord, are you going to wash my feet?"

Jesus replied, "You do not realize now what I am doing, but later you will understand."

"No," said Peter, "you shall never wash my feet."

Jesus answered, "Unless I wash you, you have no part with me."

"Then, Lord," Simon Peter replied, "not just my feet but my hands and my head as well!"

Jesus answered, "A person who has had a bath needs only to wash his feet; his whole body is clean. And you are clean, though not every one of you." For he knew who was going to betray him, and that was why he said not every one was clean.

When he had finished washing their feet, he put on his clothes and returned to his place. "Do you understand what I have done for you?" he asked them. "You call me 'Teacher' and 'Lord,' and rightly so, for that is what I am. Now that I, your Lord and Teacher, have washed your feet, you also should wash one another's feet. I have set you an example that you should do as I have done for you. I tell you the truth, no servant is greater than his master, nor is a messenger greater than the one who sent him. Now that you know these things, you will be blessed if you do them.

John 13:2–17

DISCUSS

1 How did Peter feel?

2 Why?

3 Why did Christ challenge Peter's attitude?

INDIVIDUALLY

Are your relationships predominantly "giving" or "receiving"? Put a (√) on the continuums below to show the relationship between giving and receiving in each of your situations.

	I GIVE	I RECEIVE
Spouse	_____	
Children	_____	
Parents	_____	
Work	_____	
Other Christians	_____	
Significant Friends	_____	
Church	_____	

Discuss

in groups of four
what the continuums
reveal about each of you.

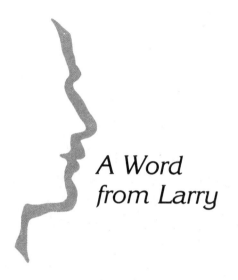

A Word from Larry

"You should wash *one another's* feet," Jesus concluded. "I have set you an example that you should do as I have done for you."

The example Jesus set is two-fold. It is first of all His call to each of us to serve others. We are to be servants, for Jesus was a servant, and we can aspire to nothing greater than to be like our Master.

But there is another aspect of this teaching. We see it in Peter's embarrassment at being served. If we are to serve *one another,* then we must each be willing to be both givers *and* receivers. We must share what we are with others, and let them share what they are with us.

This is true in every way, not simply with material things. The body of Christ grows by "that which every joint supplies," Paul says in Ephesians. We are each givers to help our brothers and sisters learn and grow, and we are each receivers from our brothers and sisters, who by sharing themselves with us help us grow.

So reach out. Give of yourself. And open up. Be willing to receive.

Go around
the room . . .

thanking others
for any ways they have
served you these three months.

INSIGHT

1 Think again about your answers to these five servant/serving items from pages 18–20.

On the left, mark each item: SA (strongly agree), A (agree), ? (uncertain), D (disagree), SD (strongly disagree).

___ 1. A Christian ought always to serve others and not ___ consider his own needs. (30.)
___ 2. A Christian should give more than he receives. ___ (32.)
___ 3. One should take care of himself first, so he has ___ energy to serve others. (14.)
___ 4. An immature believer will need to receive, while a ___ mature believer will be able to give. (1.)
___ 5. It is more spiritual to give than to receive. (19.) ___

On the right, mark each item: C (characterizes the kind of person I am), B (describes the kind of person I am becoming), D (does not describe me).

2 This week seek to bring a healthy balance to one of the relationship areas you marked on page 113.

PRESENT AND FUTURE

Mark 14–15

In one passage Paul suggests "the present time
is of the utmost importance" (Rom. 13:11, PHILLIPS).
In another he speaks of "forgetting those things
which are behind" and of "pressing toward the mark
of the high calling of God in Christ Jesus" (Phil. 3:14).
In everyone's life there is a tension
between our present experiences and our future goals.
Which is to have priority? How are they to be balanced?
For the Christian there is a unique, added dimension!

RECALL

an experience, as a child or adolescent,
where you either

1 chose to put off a
   desire for something *"now"*
   to gain a longer range goal, or

2 chose a "now" experience
   or thing instead of a
   longer range goal.

SHARE

that experience in groups of eight.
Be sure to include *how
you felt afterward* and also
anything you *learned from the
experience.*

INDIVIDUALLY

Are you facing any decisions now in which you must decide between present and future benefits? If so . . . jot down the decision
and the issues you have to consider.

_____

_____

_____

_____

_____

_____

_____

_____

_____

_____

_____

_____

SHARE
with the others.

Take notes on decisions
other group members now face:

_____

_____

_____

_____

_____

_____

·_____

_____

_____

_____

_____

READ TOGETHER

The Bible tells us Jesus determined to choose
God's will rather than any other pathway. For Jesus
that basic decision led to a tragic "present"
experience, as recorded in the following events.
Below each passage *jot down* those things Jesus
had to cope with in His present. We've completed
the first one for you.

Then Judas Iscariot, one of the Twelve, went to the chief priests to betray Jesus
to them. They were delighted to hear this and promised to give him money. So
he watched for an opportunity to hand him over.

Mark 14:10–11

a follower's betrayal

They went to a place called Gethsemane, and Jesus said to his disciples, "Stay
here while I pray." He took Peter, James and John along with him, and he began
to be deeply distressed and troubled. "My soul is overwhelmed with sorrow to
the point of death," he said to them. "Stay here and keep watch." Going a little
farther, he fell to the ground and prayed that if possible the hour might pass
from him. "Abba, Father," he said, "everything is possible for you. Take this cup
from me. Yet not what I will, but what you will."

Mark 14:32–36

They all condemned him as worthy of death. Then some began to spit at him; they blindfolded him, struck him with their fists, and said, "Prophesy!" And the guards took him and beat him.

Mark 14:64–65

The soldiers led Jesus away into the palace (that is, the Praetorium) and called together the whole company of soldiers. They put a purple robe on him, then wove a crown of thorns and set it on him. And they began to call out to him, "Hail, King of the Jews!" Again and again they struck him on the head with a staff and spit on him. Falling on their knees, they worshiped him. And when they had mocked him, they took off the purple robe and put his own clothes on him. Then they led him out to crucify him.

Mark 15:16–20

In the same way the chief priests and the teachers of the law mocked him among themselves. "He saved others," they said, "but he can't save himself! Let this Christ, this King of Israel, come down now from the cross, that we may see and believe." Those crucified with him also heaped insults on him.

Mark 15:31–32

At the sixth hour darkness came over the whole land until the ninth hour. And at the ninth hour Jesus cried out in a loud voice, "Eloi, Eloi, lama sabachthani?"—which means, "My God, my God, why have you forsaken me?"

Mark 15:33–34

TOGETHER
BRAINSTORM

What did Christ's obedience in a "difficult present" lead to? Think of as many positive results as you can.

_____

_____

_____

_____

_____

_____

_____

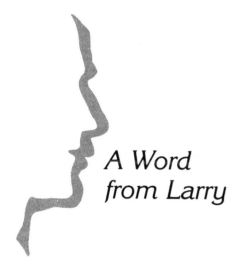

A Word
from Larry

Christ's choice of obedience led Him toward a significant future . . . through a present of suffering.

It's not always like that for us. In fact, Peter teaches that the most likely result of choosing and following God's will is a blessed present. It's only in the unusual case where doing right leads to suffering (1 Peter 3:13–14).

But there is one significant difference between Jesus' experience and our own in addition to the intensity of His suffering. For Jesus the outcome was *known.* Thus the Bible says that "for the joy that was set before him he endured the cross," and

Jesus told His disciples beforehand about His coming resurrection. You and I *can not know what our present choices will lead us to.* We do not know the future.

What we, as Christians, do know is a God who holds the future in His Hand.

This is why decision making for Christians is not a matter of balancing today's choices against hoped for or expected outcomes. It is a matter of responsiveness to God's leading, as He directs us in our present into His path for us.

There is certainly a mystical and supernatural dimension to discerning God's will. He speaks to us in many different ways. But there is also a very practical dimension as well. The better we know God, the more we share His perspective on life, the more clearly we will be able to sense His leading.

That's why a study of Christian values is so important. We need to be able to evaluate life from His point of view. When what is truly important to me are the same things that are truly important to God, I have taken significant strides in my present toward a truly significant and fulfilling future.

READ

Marie knew the minute Allen came in the door that something important had happened. "Guess what!" he exclaimed. "I've been offered a promotion to regional manager, in Albuquerque. It means a big raise, too. And they want me there in thirty days. What do you think about that!"

"I think I want to sit down," Marie said. "Wow."

And then, frowning, she began to think out loud about their church, the people they'd met in the neighborhood, the children's school, and . . .

DISCUSS

1 What are some of the values that Marie and Allen will want to consider in determining God's will?

2 If time allows, also explore one or more of the decisions you face (p. 122).

INSIGHT

1 Think again about your answers to these five present/future items from pages 18–20.

On the left, mark each item: SA (strongly agree), A (agree), ? (uncertain), D (disagree), SD (strongly disagree).

___ 1. Everyone should put away 15% of his income for ___ future emergencies. (10.)

___ 2. A Christian should live in the present and never be ___ concerned for the future. (26.)

___ 3. A person who makes wise decisions will always ___ consider the future outcome. (35.)

___ 4. We should always live for eternity and not be con- ___ cerned about the present. (21.)

___ 5. A successful person grasps every opportunity ___ without hesitating. (37.)

On the right, mark each item: C (characterizes the kind of person I am), B (describes the kind of person I am becoming), D (does not describe me).

2 This week read the following:

Day 1. Matthew 6:33–34
Day 2. Philippians 3:13–15
Day 3. 2 Timothy 4:10
Day 4. Colossians 3:1–2
Day 5. Philippians 4:8–9
Day 6. Philippians 3:7–11

3 Take your own decision described on page 122 and do a values analysis as you did with the Marie/Allen situation.

CONTEXT FOR VALUES DEVELOPMENT

Values are *not* fixed. Our values, as every other aspect of our personalities, have the potential for growth and for change. But sometimes people do not seem able or willing to change. Even when change means growth.

One reason for resistance to growth is that people around us may create a context in which it is dangerous to explore or to be different. In a context like that little change in values will take place. And, on the other hand, where a warm and loving community that provides support and freedom to explore exists, growth and change in values are more likely.

This is one of the most important things to understand about the Christian church. The church is not a place, an institution, or a set of programs. The church of Christ is a family of brothers and sisters; a community. A community designed by God as a context for our transformation.

EVALUATE

your group as a context
for values growth.

Belonging: In a true community there is a deepening sense of belonging. We know that we are loved. And we love others. We identify ourselves with the others: we belong to them and they belong to us. In a very real way we are one.

Circle the words which describe your experience of this group.

superficial	cold
open	loving
friendly	outsider
personal	close
argumentative	critical
warm	supportive
team	isolated
caring	

TELL
each other
the words you circled
and why.

EVALUATE

Dialogue: For values growth and change there must be talk about values issues. In a community like that which the church is to be, this talk can be honest and open. We can express the reality of our lives, even when this involves doubts or failures. In the openness encouraged by the loving community, barriers to growth will go down.

Have we rung the bell in this area?

Put an X on the level that represents the degree of reality in sharing and expression that you have reached. That others have reached.

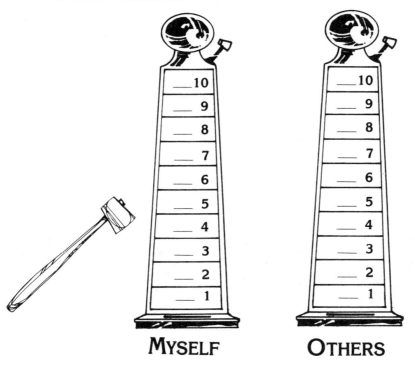

MYSELF   OTHERS

TELL
each other
the level you
checked, and
why.

Evaluate

Basic commitment: The Christian community is unique because our relationship is family: as believers we are children of God and thus brothers and sisters. We also differ in that we have a common commitment. We seek to grow closer to Christ and be responsive to His Word. The possession of the mind of Christ, ours in Scripture and in Spirit, gives us a unique basis for building common values.

Write a statement of your perception of your own and the group's commitment.

_____

_____

_____

_____

_____

Read
each other
your statements—and
discuss any agreement
or disagreement.

EVALUATE

Freedom and acceptance: In a community based on family love, there is room for individual differences. There is also room for trying—and failing. We do not demand conformity or compliance from others as the price of acceptance. In this context of freedom to explore (and even fail) we can risk the new and different thought or understanding or action. In this relational climate growth takes place—growth in values and in every other way.

Check the statements which are true of you.

____ I feel I could be myself in this group.
____ I feel free to express differing points of view than others.
____ I feel acceptance from each member of the group.
____ I feel comfortable looking at things in different ways than I had before.
____ I feel love and concern for the people with whom I disagreed.
____ I feel no pressure to insist people agree with my conclusions.
____ I feel I can trust the members of this group.

Tell each other any items you did *not* check . . . and why.

INSIGHT

1 Apply what you've been learning to your present family situation. Ask yourself or family members to do these same evaluation activities (pp. 132–137).

2 What does that evaluation suggest about your family? Directions for your own family relationships? Changes in your own thinking or understanding?

ON THE GROW 13

Values are not fixed, unchangeable aspects of anyone's personality. Oh, we can harden into fixed values, even as a person settles into only one way of thinking and closes his mind to others. But it doesn't need to happen. Especially to Christians. You see, we are being transformed! Our "minds"—and that Greek word in Romans 12 includes values—are being renewed.

So, it's good to look at our values, as you've been doing together. Each of us as a Christian wants to remain open to God, and to let ourself grow toward His image.

It *is* exciting to be a Christian. We can see ideals toward which we yearn to grow. We can even see progress toward those goals! And how good it is to know we're growing!

LOOK

at these
"values in conflict" continuums.
Place an X along the line
where you believe
God's ideal to be.

FREEDOM   CONTROL

PEOPLE   POSSESSIONS

PERSONAL GROWTH   CONFORMITY

SUCCESS   "SUCCESS"

Look
at these
"values in tension" continuums.
Place an X along the line
where you believe
God's ideal to be.

WORK _____ LEISURE

FAIRNESS _____ GRACE

IMMEDIATE GRATIFICATION _____ LONG-TERM GOALS

SERVED _____ SERVING

Go back to
pages 140 and 141
and put a O
along the continuums
to show where you
were six months
ago.

Go back to pages
140 and 141 and
put a ✔ along the
continuums to show
where you *are* now.

SHARE

Spend your last session sharing one or two
of the continuums *which indicate the
greatest change in your life.*

Share what God has been doing in your
lives, and close in prayer.